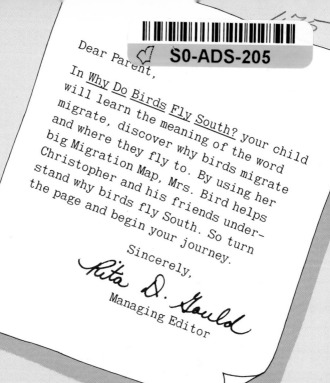

Dear Parent,

In <u>Why Do Birds Fly South?</u> your child will learn the meaning of the word migrate, discover why birds migrate and where they fly to. By using her big Migration Map, Mrs. Bird helps Christopher and his friends understand why birds fly South. So turn the page and begin your journey.

Sincerely,

Rita D. Gould

Managing Editor

FAMILY FUN

- Set up a bird feeder. Make a simple platform feeder with your child and place it on a pole outside a window. Help your child place birdseed, suet, and peanut butter on the feeder. Try to identify the birds that come to feed and share this information with your child.

- Learn your state bird. Take your child to a local library to find information about your state bird—what it is, what it looks like, the kind of nest it builds. Keep a chart to show how many times your child spots the state bird.

READ MORE ABOUT IT

- *Why Do Leaves Change Color?*
- *Why Do Animals Sleep Through Winter?*
- *Why Do Birds Sing?*

This book is a presentation of Weekly Reader
Books. Weekly Reader Books offers book
clubs for children from preschool through high
school. For further information write to:
WEEKLY READER BOOKS, 4343 Equity Drive,
Columbus, Ohio 43228

This edition is published by arrangement
with Checkerboard Press.

Weekly Reader is a federally registered trademark
of Field Publications.

WEEKLY READER BOOKS presents

Why Do Birds Fly South?

A **Just Ask**™ Book

Hi, my name is Christopher!

by Chris Arvetis
and Carole Palmer

illustrated by
Dick Smolinski

FIELD PUBLICATIONS
MIDDLETOWN, CT.

This spring we came
here to live.
We built our nests and
made our homes.
We had our babies.
All summer it was
warm and nice.
It was easy to find food.

Then the days started
to get shorter.
There was less sunlight.
It got much cooler.
That tells us winter
is coming.
And it is time to leave.

We fly south where it is warm.
We need to live in a warm place where we can find food.
When birds fly south for the winter, we say they migrate.

Now, we are ready to migrate.
Birds migrate in different ways.
Some birds fly alone.
Others fly in big groups
called flocks.

CANADA

UNITED
STATES

MEXICO

Let's look at a map and see where birds travel.

Canada geese fly together in flocks.

They start here and travel only a short way.

They want a warmer place where they can find food.

When it turns cold, wrens and bluebirds gather in flocks and fly south, too.

They travel to warm places for the winter months.

Time to leave!

Black crows also
fly south.
And so do many of the
blue jays and redwing
blackbirds.

The tiny hummingbirds start
in the north.
Most of them follow this path.
They can even travel over part
of an ocean without stopping.
Each year, the little birds
travel 3,000 miles.

Some birds seem to use mountains and coastlines to keep on the right path.

They seem to use the sun to help them know which way to go.

Other birds seem to use the night stars to guide them as they migrate.

People who study birds have put
bands on our legs to find out
where we migrate.
People have learned where we go,
how we go, and how long it takes.
Why do birds know when to migrate?
How do they find their way?
People can only guess.

When spring comes we know
it is time to fly back north to build
our nests and have our babies.

Then the days get shorter
and cooler.

There is less sunlight.

So…what do we do
all over again?

12/5